YOU'RE WAITING ON YOU

YOU'RE WAITING ON YOU

WHY *REAL* RECOVERY STARTS WITH YOU— NOT THEM

A GUIDE FOR FAMILIES STRUGGLING WITH ADDICTION AND RELAPSE

BROOK MCKENZIE

For the ones who lost themselves trying to save someone else.

*"When we are no longer able to change a situation,
we are challenged to change ourselves."*
— Viktor E. Frankl

CONTENTS

SECTION ONE | 1
WAKING UP TO REALITY

SECTION TWO | 25
BREAKING THE PATTERN

SECTION THREE | 51
REDEFINING LOVE AND LETTING GO

SECTION FOUR | 77
LIVING FREE

FOREWORD

Over the years, I've worked with thousands of families facing addiction. Some were just beginning to make sense of the chaos. Others were years deep—exhausted, confused, and clinging to the hope that the next treatment, the next breakthrough, might finally be the one. Most of them had tried everything *except* the one thing that truly makes the difference: changing themselves. What families need isn't more theory. It's not another soft suggestion to "set a boundary" or "practice self-care." They need clarity, direction, and the courage to stop waiting.

That's exactly what this book delivers.

I've known Brook for a long time, and what's always stood out is his clarity, steadiness, and lived understanding of what real recovery demands—not just from the addicted loved one, but from the entire family system. Like me, he's experienced it firsthand. And like me, he's spent years helping others walk through it. In my work as an interventionist, I've seen the same patterns play out across thousands of families—good people stuck in fear, guilt, and confusion, waiting for something to change. What they need is a way forward.

You're Waiting on You actually gives them one. It's like sitting down for a one-hour intervention in book form. It's fast, clear, and cuts straight to the core of what families actually need to hear—especially in the middle of the chaos. Brook didn't waste time with theories or long-winded explanations. He wrote it like a rapid-fire string of hard truths—one after another, clear, direct, and impossible to ignore. You can read a chapter in five minutes and carry it with you the rest of the day. And when you're in the trenches, that's exactly what you need.

If you're reading this, you're probably scared, exhausted, and desperate to make the right move. You might be thinking: *What else can I do? What if I do the wrong thing? What if it's too late?* I've heard it all. And what I can tell you, after years of walking families through this process, is that the answer isn't found in rescuing, fixing, or softening the consequences. It's not in loving harder or explaining more clearly. It's in letting go of fear-based rescuing, expecting more from the addicted loved one, and choosing the kind of discomfort that leads to change.

This book lays it out plainly. The transformation doesn't start with them. It starts with you. When families begin to hold boundaries, speak the truth, and step out of emotional chaos, everything shifts. Addiction thrives in dysfunction. Recovery begins with clarity—and sometimes, that clarity has to come from you first.

In my own journey—both personally and professionally—I've seen what happens when families stop waiting and start leading. The principles you'll find in this book are the same ones I live by in my work with families across the country.

Brook has lived this. I've lived this. You're not alone. But you're also not off the hook. As the title says: *You're Waiting on You.*

Let's begin.

Sam Davis

Drug and Alcohol Interventionist

PREFACE

I didn't set out to write a book. I set out to survive the heartbreak of addiction—and to help others survive it, too.

For several years, I've worked with families caught in the chaos of a loved one's addiction. Desperate parents. Exhausted spouses. Siblings who don't know whether to stay close or step away. People who love deeply but are drowning in fear, guilt, and confusion.

They come looking for help—for the addicted loved one.
> They want to fix what's broken, stop the bleeding, and finally get through to the person they love.
> They hope there's a key. A method. A phrase. Something that will turn the corner for good.

But somewhere underneath that desperation is something else.
> A quiet ache.
> A dawning awareness.
> A sense that maybe the old way of helping is part of the problem.

And eventually, the real question emerges:
> **What if changing them isn't the answer?**
> **What if I'm the one who needs to change first?**

That's where this book begins.

This book was born out of thousands of very real, and very personal family engagements. Not theories. Not clinical white papers. Real conversations with real families in real pain. It's written for people who have tried everything, who are worn down, and who are finally ready to embrace something different—even if it's hard.

What I've learned, over and over again, is this: the family matters. The family has power. The family can heal—regardless of what the addicted person chooses to do.

But healing won't come from fixing the addicted loved one. It won't come from managing chaos, controlling outcomes, or rescuing someone from their own consequences.

Healing comes when you start telling the truth. When you stop negotiating with dysfunction. When you raise the bar—not just for them, but for yourself. When you stop trying to feel better, and start learning how to get better.

Because sometimes, the most loving thing you can do for them—is to get better without them.

And when you do, you won't just survive.
    You'll get free.
    You'll get well.

And maybe, just maybe, they will too.

—Brook McKenzie

WHY LOVE ISN'T ENOUGH

THERE'S A KIND of heartbreak only a family knows.

It's not just watching someone you love destroy their life.
It's watching them do it *again*.

It's holding onto hope long after everyone else gave up.
It's writing the check, planning the intervention, taking the midnight call—only to be lied to, manipulated, or stood up time and again.

It's the sleepless nights.
The double life.
The chaos.
The silence.
The endless cycles of crisis, fear, and guilt.

It's not just loving the addicted individual.

It's loving them so much you start to lose yourself.

I've lived it.

Not as the parent or the spouse—but as the addicted person.

The one no one expected much from.
The one who lied, disappeared, relapsed, and took everyone down with him—again and again.
The one whose family didn't know what else to do.

And I got well.

Not because I was finally ready.
Not because someone said the perfect words.
But because the people around me stopped managing my emotions—and started telling the truth.
They let me face consequences. They let me hurt. They let me choose.

And that choice saved my life.

Over the years, I've sat with thousands of families just like yours.
I've listened to the desperate questions:
"Is this ever going to work?"
"Are we helping or enabling?"
"What else can we possibly do?"
I've watched parents blame themselves, marriages unravel, siblings vanish into silence.

Maybe that's where you are now.

If so, I want to tell you something that's always learned the hard way:
You're not waiting on them.
You're waiting on you.

This book is not about fixing your loved one.
It's about waking up your family.
It's about breaking the trance.

It's about telling the truth—out loud, all the way, without flinching.

WHY THIS BOOK IS FOR THE FAMILY

There are a thousand books written for the addicted.
Memoirs. Treatment models. Recovery tools.

And yes—some of them are beautiful, raw, and important.

But what about the families?

What about the mothers whose nervous systems have been hijacked by fear?
What about the fathers stuck in a silent, frozen kind of pain?
What about the siblings who quietly disappear because they're tired of being invisible?
What about the marriages buckling under the weight of chaos?

This book is for them.
This book is for *you.*

Not to teach you how to love better—but how to *love differently.*
Not to help you hold on tighter—but to help you *let go with clarity.*
Not to give you false hope—but to give you back your own life.

THE CORE MESSAGE

This book has one central message, and I'll say it plainly:

You are powerless over the addicted loved one.

But **you are not powerless over your life.**

You don't control their readiness.
    You can't force their surrender.
    You're not in charge of the outcome.

But you are allowed to get well—even if they don't.
    You are allowed to detach—even if they call it betrayal.
    You are allowed to live—even while they're still lost.

And the most important work—the work that changes everything—**starts with you.**

Because here's what I believe with all my heart:
    When families change first,
    the addicted loved one has a chance.

A chance to experience **boundaries instead of bargaining.**
    A chance to feel **consequences instead of cushions.**
    A chance to meet **reality—and choose something new.**

But too often, we don't give them that chance.
    We expect too little—because we're afraid they'll break.
    We lower the bar until there's nothing left to trip over.
    We soften the truth, and call it love.
    We steal the struggle they need to grow.
    We protect them from the pain that could save their life.

And slowly, without realizing it,
    we teach them they can't.
        Can't face it.
        Can't own it.
        Can't change.

But here's the truth:

They can do hard things.
They can feel hard feelings.
And they must—**if they're ever going to recover.**

When we interrupt their pain,
we interrupt their potential.

When we shield them from consequences,
we rob them of dignity.

When we expect nothing,
we teach them they are not capable.

This isn't compassion.
It's fear.

And **fear has been running the show for too long.**

You don't need another strategy.

You need truth.
You need permission.
**You need a way forward that doesn't require you to
destroy yourself - or them - out of love.**

That's what this book is for.

Because I've watched families go from **burned out to brave.**
From **helpless to honest.**
From **twisted up in guilt to grounded in grace.**

Not by fixing their addicted loved one.
But by facing the truth about what actually works—and
what doesn't.

If you're ready for that, keep reading.
We're just getting started.

SECTION ONE

WAKING UP TO REALITY

The shift from focusing on their behavior to examining your own.

CHAPTER 1

THE MIRROR TEST

This book isn't about your loved one.

It's about *you*.

That might feel like a betrayal. After all, you picked up this book because someone you love is destroying their life. Maybe they're on their fourth treatment stay. Maybe they've lied to you again, disappeared again, stolen from you again. Maybe you're scared they won't live through the month.

And maybe—if you're honest—you're starting to wonder if *you* will either.

So let me be clear:
   Yes, addiction is real. Yes, it's devastating. Yes, your loved one needs help.

But here's the truth most people won't tell you:
   You need help too.

Not because you're a bad parent, or sibling, or partner.
   Not because you caused this.

Not even because you've done anything "wrong."

But because addiction doesn't just infect the addicted loved one. It infects the system around them. And if that system doesn't change, *nothing will.*

THE REAL REASON YOU'RE STUCK

Most families I've worked with have already done a lot.

They've cried, prayed, threatened, paid, rescued, researched, intervened, begged. They've sent their loved one to rehab. They've gotten them a therapist. They've done everything they know how to do—and a hundred things they never thought they'd have to.

But underneath it all is a hidden pattern. A silent contract the family has made with reality:
"I'll do anything to help… as long as I don't have to change."

This is where we begin. With a mirror.
Not for your loved one—for you.

Because if you're still here, still reading, you probably know what I'm about to say next:
They aren't changing. So you have to.

THE INVISIBLE ADDICTION

Addicted loved ones are easy to spot.
But the family's version of addiction is more subtle. It doesn't always show up as bottles, pills, or needles. It shows up as patterns:

- Controlling conversations
- Walking on eggshells
- Covering for missed responsibilities
- Giving money when you swore you wouldn't
- Stalking social media to find out where they are
- Rationalizing behavior you know is insane

None of that feels like addiction.

It feels like *love*.

But it's not.

It's fear. It's grief. It's guilt. It's the need to *do something* to avoid feeling powerless.

And just like the addicted person who reaches for the next hit, **you reach for relief.**

WHO DO YOU BECOME IN CRISIS?

Here's a question to ask yourself:

When your loved one is in crisis, who do you become?

Do you become the fixer?

The investigator?

The rescuer?

The silent enabler?

The anxious controller?

This is where your work begins. Not with them—but with *your response to them.*

Because your role in this system—your identity in it—has become part of the problem. And it's kept you trapped just as surely as they are.

You can't free them by changing them.

But you *can* stop playing the role you've been cast in.

THE BRAVEST MOVE YOU CAN MAKE

I don't say any of this to shame you. If you knew better, you'd be doing better. But *no one* talks to families this way. You've been told to support, encourage, maybe set a boundary or two. But you've rarely been told this:

You're in your own kind of denial.

You've avoided the truth that's been in front of you for a long time:
You are stuck. And you're not stuck because of your loved one's addiction.
You're stuck because of your own resistance to change.

That's the brave move now: to stop trying to change someone who won't...

and start changing the only person who *can*.

You.

THE MIRROR DOESN'T LIE

This chapter isn't here to offer solutions. It's here to offer a moment of recognition. A pause. A mirror. And what you see in it may be painful—but it's also your way out.

You don't have to keep trying the same things.

You don't have to keep rescuing.

You don't have to keep suffering in the background of someone else's story.

You can write a new story.

One where your peace, your clarity, and your transformation aren't dependent on whether they change.

But it all starts with this question:

What have I been unwilling to face about myself?

That's the mirror test.

And it's where everything begins.

CHAPTER 2

COMFORT IS THE DRUG

I've sat with families in every state you can imagine: hopeful, hopeless, skeptical, outraged, broken open. They come after the fifth, seventh, twelfth relapse, saying things like:

"We just want him to get better."

"We've tried everything."

"We don't know what else to do."

And almost every time, I want to ask a question they're not expecting:

What are you doing to avoid your own discomfort?

Most families think this work is about the addicted loved one. But real transformation starts when the family realizes that **their own behavior is driven by the same thing that fuels addiction: the need for relief.**

The addicted individual drinks or uses to feel better. The family fixes, rescues, explains, begs, and pays for treatment—*to feel better.*

Let's call it what it is: **comfort is the family's drug of choice.**

THE CYCLE OF RESCUE AND RELAPSE

I once worked with a father who had bailed his daughter out of jail six times. She was 27, addicted to fentanyl and alcohol, and had burned every bridge you can name—job, school, relationship, family. Every time she landed in jail, he swore it was the last. Every time, he bailed her out.

When I asked why, he said:
"I can't stand the thought of her in there. I just… I can't take it."

That's the problem. He wasn't trying to rescue *her*—he was trying to escape *himself*. Escape the guilt. The fear. The unbearable what-ifs. He was desperate to feel better.

But the hard truth is this: **when your priority is to feel better, you will never get better.** Not as a family. Not as a parent. Not as a system.

Addiction is sustained by behavior. And when families act out of emotional discomfort, they unknowingly become *co-conspirators* in the very disease they're trying to destroy.

YOU'RE NOT HELPING—YOU'RE COPING

Most families who say "We're doing everything we can," mean they're doing everything that feels helpful.

But what feels helpful isn't always what *is* helpful.
And what actually helps—boundaries, silence, detachment—often feels *awful*.

So most families don't do it.

They'll say "We're scared for his life," but what they really mean is:

"We're scared to feel powerless."

"We're scared to grieve."

"We're scared to say no and be hated for it."

But recovery—real recovery—doesn't begin with comfort.

It begins with *clarity and courage.*

THE ADDICTION YOU DIDN'T NOTICE

This isn't about blame. It's about awareness.

No one taught you this. You didn't know you were enabling. You were loving. You were protecting.

But over time, the addicted loved one learns to control the system with precision—because the system is soft where it hurts.

They use your fear.

They use your guilt.

They use your love.

And because you don't want to feel shame or sadness or helplessness, you step in. You fix. You chase. You hope. You rescue. And the cycle begins again.

Until someone in the system—*you*—decides to do something different.

TRUTH IS NOT COMFORTABLE

So here's the shift that has to happen:

You must stop trying to feel better.

You must start telling the truth.

You will not feel better in the short term. In fact, if you are truly changing your role in this system, you're going to feel worse. That's how you'll know it's working.

You will feel grief when you stop controlling.
You will feel fear when you stop fixing.
You will feel pain when you let consequences play out.

But pain is not the enemy. Avoidance is.

ASK THIS INSTEAD

Families often ask:
"How can we help him stop?"

But the better question is:
"How can we stop doing what we do to avoid discomfort?"

Because if you can answer that—and act on it—you change the entire dynamic. You stop being a participant in the sickness. You start being a presence that's grounded, real, and healthy.

That might not save the addicted loved one.

But it will stop destroying *you*.

And sometimes, when you finally stop participating in the game, the addicted person has no one left to perform for.

CHAPTER 3

THE GUILT LIE

Guilt is the most convincing liar in the family system.

It whispers:

"You failed them."

"This is your fault."

"You owe them another chance."

"If you hadn't ____, they wouldn't be this way."

"You can't turn your back on your own child."

And maybe the most dangerous lie of all:

"If you really loved them, you wouldn't let them suffer."

Let me be clear: guilt is not love.

It's fear, dressed up as responsibility.

And as long as guilt is driving the car, don't expect the destination to change.

GUILT FEELS RIGHT—BUT IT'S A TRAP

Families stuck in the cycle of addiction almost always operate from guilt. Not all the time, not every decision—but often enough that it becomes a pattern.

- You set a boundary... then feel guilty and backtrack.
- You say no... then lose sleep and change your mind.
- You try to detach... then worry you're being "cold."
- You protect them from consequences... then feel ashamed of your own exhaustion.

This is what guilt does. It confuses clarity. It disguises enabling. It paralyzes action.

And the addicted loved one learns—consciously or not—how to *leverage* your guilt. They don't have to manipulate. You'll do it to yourself.

WHERE GUILT COMES FROM

Guilt comes from three core places:

1. **The belief that you caused this**

   Maybe you made mistakes. Maybe there were things you didn't see soon enough. Maybe the marriage ended, or the home wasn't perfect, or there was trauma you couldn't prevent. So you carry this quiet, lingering sense that it's all somehow your fault.

2. **The belief that you failed to fix it**

   You've sent them to treatment. You've supported them through job losses, arrests, overdoses. You've done *so much*. But nothing is working. So now the guilt says: "You're not just a failure as a parent—you're failing at recovery too."

3. **The belief that love means protection**

   If they suffer, you've failed. That's the lie. So you keep trying to shield them from the consequences of their choices—because the pain feels unbearable. But in trying to protect them, you're often protecting them *from the very experiences they need to grow.*

THE HARD TRUTH

You didn't cause this.
   You can't control it.
   And you can't cure it.

You've heard that before. Maybe in a family group or pamphlet. But here's the part they don't always say:
   You also don't need to *atone* for it.

Your guilt is not required.
   Your punishment is not required.
   And your refusal to suffer doesn't make you heartless.

It makes you *clear.*

You cannot love your child (or spouse, or sibling) into recovery.
   But you can love them *without carrying guilt for choices they continue to make.*

GUILT IS A TERRIBLE GUIDE

When you let guilt steer your decisions, you become reactive, inconsistent, and emotionally entangled.

You say "no" on Monday, "maybe" on Wednesday, and "fine" by Friday.

Not because you're weak. Because you're human—and guilt is exhausting. It wears you down until *relief* feels like the only way out.

But the goal here is not relief. The goal is truth.

And the truth is this: you can feel guilt—and still hold the line.

You can love deeply—and still say no.

You can acknowledge your past—and still choose something different now.

A NEW QUESTION

When families ask me what to do, I often tell them to stop asking,
"What's the right thing to do?"
and instead ask,
"What would I do if I wasn't feeling guilty?"

That question changes everything.

It gets you out of emotion and into clarity.
It grounds you in the present.
And it reminds you: guilt is a feeling—not a compass.

YOU DON'T OWE THEM MORE CHANCES

This is the hardest line in the chapter, but it needs to be said:
You don't owe your loved one unlimited chances.

Love is not infinite accommodation.
Boundaries are not cruelty.
And consequences are not abandonment.

If your loved one wants to get well, they will find a way.
If they don't, no amount of guilt will make them.

What they need is not a parent wrapped in shame.
They need someone who is *willing to stand in truth,* even
when it hurts.

And that's what you can become.

CHAPTER 4

FEAR-BASED PARENTING: A BLUEPRINT FOR FAILURE

You know the fear. It wakes you up at 2:00 a.m.

It tightens your chest every time the phone rings.

It whispers:

"What if he dies?"

"What if this is the last chance?"

"What if I say the wrong thing and lose her forever?"

Fear is understandable.

It's real.

But when it becomes the driving force behind your parenting—or your partnership—it will guide you to do the exact opposite of what's needed.

Fear-based parenting doesn't protect your child.

It paralyzes you.

And in the process, it protects the addiction.

FEAR MASQUERADING AS LOVE

Parents tell me:
"I just want him to be okay."
"I don't want her to hate me."
"I'm scared that if we cut her off, we'll lose her forever."

That's not love.
That's fear with a mask on.

When you parent from fear, everything becomes about short-term relief:

- Avoiding the blow-up
- Calming the chaos
- Preventing a relapse
- Keeping them alive at all costs

And yes, the desire to keep your child alive is real.
But when *your fear of loss becomes louder than your clarity*, you're not making decisions—you're *reacting*.

HOW FEAR SHOWS UP

Fear doesn't always look like panic. Sometimes it's much more subtle:

- **Over-explaining:** Trying to get the addicted person to "see" or "understand"
- **Soft boundaries:** Saying no but hinting yes
- **Emotional bribery:** "Don't you see how much you're hurting me?"
- **Avoiding consequences:** "This time is different. He really means it."

- **Constant checking in:** Making sure they're still sober, still safe, still okay

These don't seem like fear-based behaviors. But they are.

Because deep down, you're afraid:
If I don't do something… something terrible will happen.

That's the lie.
And addiction *loves* that lie.
Because as long as fear controls you, addiction controls the system.

FEAR IS A TERRIBLE STRATEGY

Fear doesn't produce strength.
It produces inconsistency.

You say one thing on Monday, change your mind by Thursday. You hold a hard line, then let it slide the moment you hear, "I'm trying, I promise."

It's not because you're weak.
It's because you're terrified.
But parenting through terror leads to one result: collapse.

Fear keeps you negotiating with insanity.
Fear keeps you micromanaging a disease you don't control.
Fear keeps you more focused on *not losing them* than *requiring them to show up as someone worth keeping.*

THE ILLUSION OF CONTROL

Here's the real mind trick: fear convinces you that you're doing something helpful.

That calling every morning, reminding them of appointments, tracking their location, checking their bank account—these are all acts of "love."

They're not.

They're *attempts to control the uncontrollable.*

Because the truth is too painful to face:
"I can't make them change. I can't make them choose life. I can't make them value what I value."

So we scramble.
We helicopter.
We compromise our boundaries.
And we call it love.

COURAGE IS QUIET

What does real courage look like in parenting a child with addiction?

- It's holding the boundary when your heart is breaking.
- It's saying "no" and sitting in the silence that follows.
- It's refusing to chase, to fix, or to explain your decision one more time.
- It's grieving who they are today without abandoning who you are.
- It's letting them walk away—and not following.

Courage isn't loud.
It doesn't come with applause.
But it is the only force stronger than fear.
And it's the only place real leadership comes from.

CHOOSING PRINCIPLE OVER PANIC

Every family reaches a crossroads. One side is panic. The other is principle.

- Panic says, *"What if this is the last chance?"*
- Principle says, *"I won't be manipulated by fear."*
- Panic says, *"I need to do something."*
- Principle says, *"I will no longer do what doesn't work."*
- Panic says, *"They'll hate me."*
- Principle says, *"I can love you even while you're mad at me."*

This is the shift.

This is where everything starts to change.

When your fear no longer dictates your behavior, your child may finally have to face *the truth of theirs.*

FINAL WORD

You will still feel fear.

Of course you will.

But your job is not to *eliminate* fear.

Your job is to stop letting fear lead.

Let something deeper take the lead now:

Truth.

Clarity.

Conviction.

Love—real love—not the kind that rescues, but the kind that holds the line.

They may not change.

But you can.

And when you do, everything changes.

SECTION TWO
BREAKING THE PATTERN

*Recognizing and dismantling the hidden
agreements that keep everyone stuck.*

CHAPTER 5

THE UNSPOKEN DEAL: "DON'T MAKE ME FEEL THAT WAY AGAIN"

Most families don't realize they've made a deal with their addicted loved one.

It's not in writing. It's not even conscious. But it's there—like a shadow underneath every conversation, every decision, every relapse, every rescue.

Here's how the deal sounds:
"I'll keep helping you…
if you stop making me feel guilty."
"I'll give you another chance…
if you don't scare me with your choices."
"I'll fix your newest crisis…
if you don't break my heart again."

This is the unspoken agreement between the addicted loved one and family:

"Don't make me feel that way again."

And as long as this deal remains in place, both parties stay sick.

YOU'RE NOT CRAZY. YOU'RE IN A CONTRACT.

Have you ever:

- Said "yes" when every part of you screamed "no"?
- Backed down from a boundary just to avoid another fight?
- Apologized for your tone even though you were right?
- Offered "help" just to stop the guilt and anxiety?

That's not weakness.
That's not codependency.
That's a *contract*.

You don't want to be abandoned, hated, blamed, or rejected.
So you trade your own clarity for temporary emotional peace.

But the moment you make that trade, the addicted loved one has control.
Because now they don't have to manipulate you-you'll do it for them.

HOW IT STARTS

This dynamic often begins long before addiction becomes visible. It's rooted in something much older:

- A parent's unresolved guilt
- A history of emotional neglect
- An over-identification with the child's feelings

- Or simply the desire to avoid more pain than you think you can handle

Somewhere along the way, the addicted loved one learned that if they suffer, *you will move.*

If they cry, you soften.
> If they explode, you retreat.
> If they spiral, you clean it up.

This isn't because you're naive.
> It's because, like them, **you want relief.**
> And so the contract gets reinforced—over and over again:
> "I'll do what you want… as long as you don't make me feel that way again."

THE ADDICTED PERSON'S ROLE: VILLAIN AND VICTIM

In this deal, the addicted individual gets to be both villain *and* victim.

They hurt you—then convince you it's your fault.
> They betray you—then collapse into shame.
> They burn down the house—then cry over the ashes.
> And you… clean up again. Pay again. Make excuses again. Justify again.

Because the alternative—feeling your own pain, your own grief, your own helplessness—is unbearable.

So you stay in the loop.
> Not because you're stupid.
> Because you're *afraid.*

WHEN THEY'RE NOT THE ONLY ONE PERFORMING

The addicted loved one isn't the only one putting on a show.

Families often perform too:

- You pretend to be fine when you're not.
- You act calm when your insides are screaming.
- You say "we just want what's best for him," when the truth is "we are scared to death and barely functioning."

This performance doesn't help the addicted loved one-it *protects* the system.

Because if you were to break character—if you were to stop pretending—you'd have to face the thing no one wants to admit:
You've become a part of the sickness.

Not because you wanted to.
But because you couldn't bear to feel the truth.

THE CONTRACT ENDS WHEN YOU STOP PERFORMING

There's a moment that changes everything.

It's not dramatic.
It's not an ultimatum.
It's not a scream or a slammed door.

It's quiet.
Resolute.

It sounds like:

"I will no longer betray myself to avoid your feelings."
"You are allowed to be angry. And I am allowed to say no."
"I will feel all the things I've avoided. And I will survive them."

That's how the contract ends.

Not with a confrontation—but with a decision.
 Not with control—but with clarity.

WHAT YOU OWE, AND WHAT YOU DON'T

You do not owe your addicted loved one…

- Your silence
- Your availability
- Your money
- Your emotional regulation
- Your trust, over and over again

What you owe them is the truth:
 About yourself. About your limits. About what you will and won't participate in anymore.

You can say,
 "I love you."
 "I want you to recover."
 "But I will no longer sacrifice my well-being to protect you from the pain of your own choices."

That's not cruelty.
 That's sanity.

THE NEW DEAL

If there's a new contract to make, it's this:
"I will no longer demand that you change.
I will no longer try to outrun my pain.
I will no longer settle for survival.
I will do my work. Whether you do yours or not."

When that becomes your posture, you no longer need the old arrangement.

You're not waiting for them to get better.
You're becoming better—starting now.

CHAPTER 6

SET EXPECTATIONS. THEN ACTUALLY HOLD THEM.

Most families I work with have no idea how low their standards have dropped.

By the time they reach out, they're not hoping for their son or daughter to be responsible, accountable, or sober. They're just hoping they answer the phone. That they don't lie—*too much*. That they stay out of jail this month. That the call isn't from the coroner.

Somewhere along the way, the bar didn't just lower—it fell through the floor.

And what they don't see is that **this low bar becomes part of the addicted loved one's identity.**

"They don't expect anything from me, so I must not be capable of anything."

THE UNINTENTIONAL MESSAGE

Families don't mean to do this.

But over time, their expectations erode under the weight of relapse, manipulation, and heartbreak.

Eventually, they stop asking their loved one to do anything hard.

They stop expecting honesty, consistency, effort.

Not out of laziness. But out of fear.

- *"If I ask too much, they'll get overwhelmed."*
- *"If I push, they'll relapse."*
- *"Let's just celebrate small wins."*

Small wins matter—but not if they replace the truth.

The truth is: **your loved one is capable of more than you think.**

They just don't believe it.

And neither do you.

ENABLING IN THE NAME OF EMPATHY

We live in a therapeutic culture where everything is "trauma-informed," "compassionate," and "supportive."

I believe in compassion. I believe in trauma work.

But somewhere along the line, families started calling **avoidance** a form of love.

They stopped confronting the addicted loved one.

They stopped telling the truth.

They stopped requiring real effort.

All in the name of "keeping them safe."

But let's be honest: if they're in active addiction, they're not safe.

And neither is the family.

Empathy without accountability is not love.

It's appeasement.

WHEN EXPECTATIONS RETURN, SO DOES DIGNITY

You want to see a miracle?

Tell your addicted loved one:
"I know what you're capable of.
I'm done treating you like a fragile child.
And I will no longer reward you for surviving—when I know you were made to *transform.*"

That one shift—raising the standard—has the power to shift the whole system.

It may not change the addicted loved one overnight.
But it begins to *strip away the excuses* that keep them from becoming who they were meant to be.

And if they resist?

That's okay.

Their resistance doesn't mean the standard is wrong.
It means they're used to the system that coddled them.

It means the work is beginning.

HOW TO SET AN EXPECTATION THAT MATTERS

Most families confuse expectations with wishes.

"We hope he'll stay sober."

"We want her to get a job."

"We're trying to support him while he gets back on his feet."

Those are all *hopes*. They're not *expectations*.

An expectation sounds like this:

"If you want to live under our roof, you must be actively working a recovery program, fully accountable, and contributing to the home."

"We are no longer providing money, rides, or bailouts. If you choose to use, you do so without our support."

"You do not get access to our presence, our resources, or our energy—unless you're showing up with honesty and effort."

Expectations are clear.

They are measurable.

And—this is key—they have *consequences* when they're not met.

THE HARD PART: ACTUALLY HOLDING THEM

Most families fail here. Not because they're bad people.

Because they're exhausted. And scared. And tired of being the "bad guy."

So they say one thing—and do another.

And the addicted loved one learns (yet again) that there is no real boundary. Just noise.

But here's the truth:

> **An unenforced boundary teaches powerlessness.**
> **A consistent boundary teaches possibility.**

If you say, "We're done helping financially," and then write another check next month, *you just taught them that words don't matter.*

But if you follow through—without cruelty, without drama, just quiet, firm consistency—*you teach them what dignity looks like.*

YOU DON'T NEED TO BE HARSH—JUST HONEST

Raising the bar doesn't mean being mean.
It means being *real.*

- "I love you, and I believe in you."
- "Because I believe in you, I'm no longer going to make your life easier when you refuse to do the work."
- "This is your life. You get to decide what to do with it. I'm not going to join you in pretending you're helpless."

That's not tough love.
That's *true love.*

THE COST OF LOW EXPECTATIONS

Here's the heartbreaking truth:

> **If you don't expect anything of your loved one, you're helping them become nothing.**

When the bar is low, people shrink to meet it.

But when someone finally raises it—and holds it—they may rise.

Maybe not right away.
Maybe not at all.

But your job is not to control the outcome.
Your job is to stop participating in a system that assumes they're incapable of anything more.

The only way to find out what someone is made of…
is to stop making excuses for who they keep choosing to be.

CHAPTER 7

STOP TRYING TO FEEL BETTER

Let's just say it plainly:
This is going to hurt.

Not because you're doing something wrong.
Not because you've failed.
But because *healing hurts*—especially when you've been trying not to feel for a very long time.

Most families don't realize how addicted they've become to emotional relief.
They don't drink or use, but they're still chasing the same thing the addicted loved one is: "Make this pain go away."

- We talk instead of act.
- We rescue instead of sit still.
- We justify instead of confront.
- We rationalize instead of grieve.
- We try to *fix the addicted loved one* so we don't have to feel *what they're doing to us.*

But the medicine you really need right now isn't another plan, another call, another emotional pep talk.

The medicine is this:
You have to learn how to suffer well.

FEELING BETTER ≠ GETTING BETTER

Most families confuse relief with progress.

You feel calmer after talking to your loved one, so you think things are getting better.

They say the right things, and your anxiety drops, so you assume this time might be different.

But here's the problem:

That same cycle of momentary relief followed by devastation has happened *how many times* now?

Too many.

You're not getting better.

You're just finding creative ways to avoid feeling worse.

That's not healing. That's avoidance.

And the only thing avoidance guarantees… is that this cycle will continue.

RELIEF IS A DRUG

We don't talk enough about this, but it's real:

Relief can be just as intoxicating as alcohol.

When your phone finally rings after days of silence… relief.

When they tell you they're "going to a meeting tonight"… relief.

When they apologize and say "I mean it this time"… relief.

And what happens next?
　　You drop your guard.
　　You soften your stance.
　　You avoid the hard conversation.
　　You forget the last time you heard this same speech.

Because that relief feels good.
　　And you've needed it.

But here's the truth:
　　You cannot build a healthy life around the need to feel okay.
　　You can only build it around the willingness to feel everything.

THIS IS WHAT ENDURANCE LOOKS LIKE

Endurance isn't passive. It's not giving up. It's not "detachment" in some emotionally cold sense.

Endurance is what love *actually* looks like when you stop trying to control outcomes.

It's…

- Feeling grief and not rushing to numb it.
- Feeling shame and not begging to fix it.
- Feeling fear and still holding the boundary.
- Watching your child suffer and not stepping in to remove their pain.
- Going to bed at night not knowing if they'll ever change—and still choosing to stay in your truth.

This is the part no one wants to do.

But it's the only way out.

YOUR FEELINGS AREN'T A PROBLEM

Let's get one thing straight:

Your anxiety isn't the problem.

Your sadness isn't the problem.

Your rage, your heartbreak, your confusion—none of that is the problem.

The problem is the belief that you *shouldn't* feel this way.

That you must "get back to normal."

That you must "stay strong."

That if you were doing this right, it wouldn't hurt so much.

Nonsense.

This hurts because it matters.

This hurts because you love them.

This hurts because you've been in a war for years—and you're just now laying down the wrong weapons.

The only way to heal is to walk through the pain, not around it.

FEELING ISN'T FAILURE

Families often break down in tears and say,

"I feel like I'm falling apart."

Good.

Let it fall apart.

Because the version of you that could tolerate this dysfunction, tiptoe around this chaos, and enable this behavior without breaking down—that version was surviving, not living.

Let her go. Let him leave.
Let the strong version of you be the one who can feel every bit of the grief… and *still hold the line.*

STOP CHASING CALM

This is going to sound strange, but stay with me:

Stop trying to be okay.

Let yourself be wrecked. Let yourself weep. Let yourself fall apart in a support group, or at the kitchen table, or on the floor of your bedroom. Let the silence stretch. Let the addicted loved one get mad at you. Let the guilt come—and pass.

Because *this* is what it looks like to reclaim your soul from the disease.

The addicted person runs from pain.
That's their pattern.

Your pattern is trying to prevent pain.
Yours, theirs, everyone's.

Break the pattern.
Let it hurt. Let it burn. Let it break your heart.
And then—let it build something better than what you've been tolerating.

THE SHIFT THAT CHANGES EVERYTHING

When you stop trying to feel better, something extraordinary happens:

You get clear.
> You get consistent.
> You get your life back.

Because you're no longer reaching for something to *stop the pain.*
> You're learning to live in truth—even when that truth is brutal.

That's where strength comes from.
> That's where transformation begins.

Not in the moment you feel better.
> But in the moment you *choose not to run.*

CHAPTER 8

EMBRACE THE CONSEQUENCES YOU'VE BEEN AVOIDING

There's a moment in every family's journey with addiction where they know exactly what they need to do...

and they still don't do it.

Not because they don't care.

Not because they're in denial.

But because the next step feels like betrayal.

"If I do this, he might hate me forever."

"If we don't help, what if she ends up on the street?"

"If we let him fall... will he survive it?"

So instead, the family delays.

Softens.

Backtracks.

Compromises.

Rationalizes.

And each time they do, one thing is being avoided:

The consequence.

CONSEQUENCES ARE NOT CRUELTY

Let's say this clearly, once and for all:
> **Letting someone face the natural outcome of their behavior is not cruel.**
> **It's reality.**

Addiction thrives in unreality.
> It thrives in fantasy, avoidance, loopholes, and rescue plans.

When you remove consequences, you create a false world—one where someone can live destructively without facing the cost.

It may feel like love.
> But it's not.

It's a form of sabotage—disguised as compassion.

YOU'VE ALREADY TRIED THE OTHER WAY

If you're reading this, you've likely been here:
- You've paid for the attorney.
- You've covered the rent.
- You've picked them up from jail.
- You've given them just "one more month" at home.
- You've bought the lie—again.
- You've prayed that this time, love would be enough.

It wasn't.

Not because your love wasn't real.
> But because love without consequences is not transformative—it's anesthetizing.

You've already tried to love them *out* of addiction.

Now it's time to love them *through* the fallout.

THE COST OF PROTECTION

Every time you step in to soften a consequence, ask yourself this:
"What am I trying to prevent?"
"Whose pain am I really trying to avoid?"
"What do I believe will happen if I finally let go?"

Is it that they'll be angry?
That you'll lose the relationship?
That you'll be blamed, judged, or misunderstood?

Or is it something deeper?

That if they fall all the way down, *you* might fall apart too?

This is the truth we've been circling:
You haven't been protecting *them*.
You've been protecting yourself—from the grief, from the terror, from the helplessness you swore you'd never feel again.

And yet, the longer you avoid it, the deeper it embeds.

HOW CONSEQUENCES WORK

Consequences are not punishments.
They're teachers.

They don't guarantee change.
But they make growth *possible*.

Here's what consequences do:

- They bring reality to the surface.
- They expose denial.
- They separate words from action.
- They strip away fantasy.
- They create space for ownership.

No addicted loved one begins to recover until something they *value* is lost.

And often, families stand in the way of that loss ever reaching them.

WHEN YOU REFUSE TO LET THEM FALL

Here's the truth you already know, deep down:

If someone's life never becomes unbearable to *them*, they won't change.

If you keep carrying the weight they were meant to feel, they will let you.

Every. Single. Time.

And if you refuse to let them fall—fully, painfully, honestly— you deny them the very experience that might break the cycle.

You are not being asked to *abandon* your loved one.

You're being asked to *stop interfering with the consequences they've earned.*

BUT WHAT IF THEY DIE?

This is the fear that paralyzes so many families. It's legitimate. It's heartbreaking. And it can't be glossed over.

So let's confront it directly:

Yes, addiction can kill.
And yes, doing nothing might lead to tragedy.

But you are not choosing between death and safety.
You are choosing between two paths that both carry risk:

- One keeps you entangled in the cycle that's been slowly killing you both.
- The other offers a sliver of hope—but only through pain, consequence, and clarity.

You don't get to guarantee their safety.
But you *do* get to stop enabling their destruction.

You don't get to control the outcome.
But you *can* decide that you will no longer participate in their slow-motion suicide.

That is not abandonment.
That is integrity.

THIS IS WHERE LOVE TURNS INTO COURAGE

Love without courage is indulgent.
It wants to be liked, needed, appreciated.

But courageous love is different.

Courageous love says:

"I'm not doing this because I don't care.
I'm doing it because I care too much to lie to you anymore."

"You've shown me who you are right now. And until you show me someone different, I can't participate in this version of your life."

"I will not protect you from the truth of your choices.
I will not insulate you from the pain that might save your life."

"I love you.
But I will not carry your cross."

CONSEQUENCES AREN'T THE END—THEY'RE THE BEGINNING

This chapter isn't an invitation to stop loving.
It's an invitation to start loving in a way that might *finally* matter.

You've tried everything else.
Now try this:

Step out of the way.
Let gravity do its work.
Let pain teach.
Let loss speak.
Let reality be the force that does what you no longer can.

Sometimes the most loving thing you can do…
is to stand still, let go, and let the fall begin.

SECTION THREE

REDEFINING LOVE AND LETTING GO

*Learning how to love without control,
and live without their recovery.*

CHAPTER 9

LOVE WITHOUT RESCUE

If you strip everything else away—the guilt, the fear, the confusion—what's left at the center of the family system is usually this:

"I love them. I just want them to be okay."

And I believe that.

Your love is not in question.

But the truth is, most families confuse love with something else entirely: **rescue.**

And while love is healing, transformational, and sacred…

Rescue is corrosive.

It starts with good intentions.

It ends with everyone stuck, bitter, confused, and exhausted.

So let's say what most people won't:

If your love is always stepping in, softening the fall,

removing the consequence, managing their emotions, or taking the hit so they don't have to…
That's not love.
That's control.

LOVE THAT PROTECTS ISN'T ALWAYS LOVE THAT HELPS

Rescue says:
"I'll suffer so you don't have to."
"I'll pay so you can avoid the shame."
"I'll lie to them so your secret stays safe."
"I'll call the rehab, the sober living, the lawyer, the therapist—anything to make this right for you."

And sometimes, rescue works.
Temporarily.

It quiets the chaos.
It buys time.
It brings a moment of peace.

But what it *doesn't* do is create accountability, growth, or change.

Why?

Because **rescue assumes they can't handle the truth of their own life.**

And when you rescue someone again and again, what you're really saying is:
"I don't believe you're strong enough to face this. So I'll carry it for you."

That's not love.

That's fear—dressed up as devotion.

WHAT LOVE WITHOUT RESCUE LOOKS LIKE

Real love says:

"I see who you are today—and I know you're capable of more."

"I'm not punishing you. I'm just no longer saving you."

"If you want a different life, you'll have to earn it. I won't keep handing it to you."

"You are worthy of healing. But I won't keep lowering myself into your chaos to prove it."

This kind of love doesn't chase.

It doesn't beg.

It doesn't co-sign delusion.

It doesn't do emotional gymnastics to avoid a blow-up.

It holds steady.

It tells the truth.

It sets the bar and refuses to lower it.

That is *real love*.

And it's what most addicted loved ones have never experienced.

STOP TRYING TO BE THE EXCEPTION

There's a quiet thought that runs through almost every parent, partner, or sibling of an addicted family member:

"They'll change for me."

It's subtle, but it's there:

- "Maybe if I just say it the right way…"
- "Maybe if I'm patient enough, gentle enough, supportive enough…"
- "Maybe if I show them how much I love them, they'll finally get it."
- "Maybe if I suffer enough, they'll stop."

You're not wrong to hope.

But here's the reality:

No one ever gets well just because someone loves them enough.

If they did, your loved one would already be better.
Because you've *loved them enough*.

Now it's time to ask the real question:
"What if loving them *differently* is what makes the difference?"

IT'S NOT LOVE IF YOU'RE ABANDONING YOURSELF

Let's flip the lens for a second.

What does your love for them cost you?

- Your peace?
- Your sleep?
- Your marriage?
- Your money?
- Your self-respect?
- Your ability to enjoy your life, your other children, your purpose?

If loving them requires you to abandon yourself…
    It's not love. It's sacrifice.
    And over time, that kind of sacrifice turns into resentment, bitterness, and despair.

You are not required to destroy yourself to prove your loyalty.
    You're allowed to have boundaries.
    You're allowed to choose peace.
    You're allowed to say, "Not like this. Not anymore."

And you're allowed to *keep loving them* while you say it.

LOVE ISN'T A FEELING. IT'S A FRAMEWORK.

We've been trained to believe that love means:

- Being available
- Being soft
- Being patient
- Being "there no matter what"

But real love is much stronger—and more sacred—than that.

Real love is a *framework*.

It says:
    "In this family, honesty is required."
    "In this home, trust must be rebuilt—not assumed."
    "In this relationship, chaos will not be normalized."
    "You get to choose your behavior. And we get to choose our boundaries."

Love without rescue has clarity.
    It has limits.
    It has dignity.

And it refuses to participate in the illusion that someone is changing when they're not.

THE SHIFT

Here's what happens when you stop rescuing:

- The addicted person is left with themselves.
- Their choices stop being blurred by your interventions.
- They finally get to feel the full weight of their behavior.
- They learn, maybe for the first time, that love isn't a safety net—it's an invitation to grow.

They may lash out.
They may test your limits.
They may try every tactic they've used in the past.

That's okay.

Let the love be steady.
Let the boundaries be clear.
Let the consequences speak louder than your fear.

And say this, if you need to:
"I love you enough to stop lying to you.
I love you enough to stop saving you.
I love you enough to believe that you can choose a different path.
But I will not walk beside you while you destroy yourself."

CHAPTER 10

YOU CAN GET BETTER EVEN IF THEY DON'T

Families spend years trapped in a dangerous lie:
"My life can't get better until *they* get better."

This belief keeps you frozen.
Waiting. Hoping. Managing. Holding your breath.

It makes your peace, your health, your joy—all of it—
conditional on someone else's behavior.
Someone who is, let's be honest, consistently unstable,
dishonest, or self-destructive.

This lie becomes a leash. And you're the one wearing the collar.

So let's say the truth that will set you free:
You can heal—even if they don't.
**You can reclaim your sanity—even if they keep choosing
chaos.**
You can live in freedom—even if they never recover.

IF YOU'RE WAITING FOR THEM TO CHANGE, YOU'RE STILL IN IT

Most families say, "We've detached."

But what they really mean is, "We've taken a few steps back and now we're watching very closely, hoping they do the right thing."

That's not detachment.

That's still *orbiting the addicted loved one's life.*

It sounds like:

- "Well, we'll wait and see how he does at sober living."
- "She said she's going back to meetings—we're cautiously optimistic."
- "We're not helping right now… but if he stays clean another 30 days, we might revisit it."

In other words, *your peace is still up for negotiation.*

You're still betting on their next move.

REAL DETACHMENT MEANS LIVING AGAIN

Real detachment doesn't mean indifference.

It means *returning to your own life.*

It means:

- Making plans without waiting to see if they'll relapse.
- Enjoying dinner without checking your phone ten times.
- Laughing again.
- Praying without begging.

- Letting go of the emotional rollercoaster you've been on for years.
- Refusing to let your nervous system be held hostage by someone else's choices.

This doesn't mean you stop loving them.
It means you stop *worshiping* them.

Because when their recovery (or lack of it) becomes your religion, your own life slowly disappears.

WHAT IF YOUR HEALING IS THE BEGINNING OF THEIRS?

Families often say:
"If I step away, I'll lose him."
"If I detach, I'll push her over the edge."
"If we live our lives, he'll think we've stopped caring."

But what if the opposite is true?

What if your healing is the very thing that finally *disrupts* the system?

What if your peace breaks the trance?

What if your refusal to be emotionally manipulated is the first time they've ever had to truly *sit with themselves*?

You've tried leading with rescue.
Try leading with example.

YOU ARE NOT A BYSTANDER
IN YOUR OWN LIFE

You are not here to *watch* your son or daughter get well.
    You are here to get well yourself.
    You are here to:

- Reclaim your voice.
- Restore your dignity.
- Reconnect with your spouse, your children, your calling.
- Begin to live—not just survive.
- Stop being a side character in a story that revolves around addiction.

You're not powerless.
    You've just been overly focused.

Take the focus off of them.
    Bring it home.

To your own body.
    To your own mind.
    To your own heart.

HEALING IS A CHOICE YOU MAKE—
NOT A GIFT THEY GIVE

Here's what most families don't realize:
    You don't need their permission to get better.
    You don't need their sobriety.
    You don't need their apologies.
    You don't even need them to admit the truth.

Would those things be helpful? Sure.

But they're not prerequisites for your recovery.

What you need is a decision.

- That your peace matters.
- That your health matters.
- That your life is not on pause until they figure theirs out.

Because you've waited long enough.

YOU'RE ALLOWED TO HAVE JOY AGAIN

This might be the most radical part of all:

You're allowed to be okay—even while they're still not.

You're allowed to smile.

To travel.

To sleep.

To make memories with people who show up for life.

To stop explaining your boundaries.

To stop trying to earn their approval.

To stop proving that you're a "good mom" or "supportive partner" or "loyal sibling."

You've done enough.

Now do what no one ever gave you permission to do:

Choose yourself.

Choose healing.

Choose joy.

Not because they're doing well.

But because *you finally are.*

CHAPTER 11

CONNECTION IS NOT THE SAME AS CLOSENESS

Families often say,
> "We just want to stay connected."
> "If we set too many boundaries, we'll lose the relationship."
> "At least we're still talking…"

But let's ask something hard:
> **What's the quality of that connection?**
> **And is it actually real?**

Because if the connection is based on fear, silence, lies, performance, or managing someone else's emotions, then what you have isn't a connection.
> **You have captivity.**

And the sooner you name that, the sooner you can begin building something honest.

PERFORMING IS NOT LOVING

Here's how you know the connection isn't healthy:

- You feel like you have to tiptoe around them.
- You edit your truth so they won't get defensive.
- You pretend to trust them even though they've done nothing to earn it.
- You agree with things you don't believe.
- You accept behavior you'd never tolerate from anyone else.

That's not closeness. That's performance.

And what it produces isn't intimacy.
It's exhaustion.

WHEN CONNECTION IS BASED ON MANIPULATION

In dysfunctional family systems, "connection" often means:
"Let's keep the addicted loved one from getting angry."
"Let's avoid the confrontation."
"Let's be supportive enough to stay in their life—but not so honest that they shut us out."

But this connection comes at a price.

Every time you silence yourself to keep the peace…
Every time you soften the truth that needed to be felt…
Every time you play along just to keep them around…
You lose a piece of yourself.
And they lose a chance to change.

Eventually, you've given so many pieces away and lost so many chances for change that there's nothing left but anxiety, guilt, and confusion.

YOU CAN'T CONNECT FROM A PLACE OF FEAR

Real connection doesn't require agreement.
It doesn't require constant closeness.
It doesn't even require daily communication.

It requires truth.

And truth can't grow in an environment built on fear.

- Fear that they'll relapse.
- Fear that they'll get angry.
- Fear that they'll disappear.
- Fear that they'll reject you for good.

That fear becomes the operating system for the relationship.
And suddenly, you're not relating to *them*—you're relating to *your fear of losing them*.

That's not connection.
That's bondage.

TRUE CONNECTION CAN SURVIVE HARD TRUTH

Here's the paradox:

The thing you're avoiding—telling the truth, setting the boundary, holding the line—might be the *only* thing strong enough to build a real relationship in the long run.

Because anything built on fantasy, manipulation, or performance is already broken.

It just hasn't collapsed yet.

But when you tell the truth…
    When you stop managing their emotions…
    When you say what needs to be said without dressing it up…

Something happens.

- You stop living in fear.
- They stop controlling you with volatility.
- The relationship either rises—or it reveals what was never there.

Either way, *you're free.*

YOU ARE NOT RESPONSIBLE FOR THEIR RESPONSE

One of the greatest shifts in any family's healing journey is this:
    "I'm responsible for what I say.
    I am *not* responsible for how you take it."

Let that sink in.

You can speak with love and still be misunderstood.
    You can set a boundary and still be accused of being cruel.
    You can act in integrity and still be punished with silence, blame, or guilt.

That doesn't mean you were wrong.

It means you've stopped playing the game.

SOMETIMES, REAL CONNECTION REQUIRES DISTANCE

This will be hard to hear, but it's true:

Some people cannot connect with you until they've lost access to you.

They need the silence.

They need the distance.

They need to feel your absence so they can begin to value your presence.

And if that day never comes?

You'll know the relationship was never based on love.

It was based on what you gave them, how you made them feel, or how much of yourself you were willing to sacrifice.

You deserve more than that.

And so do they.

THE NEW STANDARD

What if the connection looked like this instead?

- "I love you enough to tell the truth."
- "I don't need to talk to you every day to stay aligned with my values."
- "This relationship will no longer be fueled by guilt, fear, or appeasement."
- "I'm willing to be misunderstood for a while in order to live in integrity."
- "I will not trade short-term closeness for long-term sickness."

This is the new standard.

Not performance.
> Not control.
> Not emotional survival.

Truth. Respect. Space. Courage.
> And yes—love.

But *real* love.
> Not the kind that keeps you tied to someone who refuses to rise.
> The kind that invites you both to stand tall—or walk away with dignity.

CHAPTER 12

THERE IS STILL HOPE—BUT IT'S NOT WHAT YOU THINK

By now, you may be wondering:
> *"If I stop rescuing… if I stop fixing… if I stop making it all okay…*
> *what's left?*
> *Is there anything left to hope for?"*

The answer is yes.

But it may not look like what you imagined.

Hope doesn't mean:

- That your son will finally call you "Mom" again, clean and sober.
- That your daughter will walk back in the door and thank you for saving her.
- That the family will be whole again, like it used to be.
- That you'll get back the years you lost.

That kind of hope—**the bargaining kind**—keeps families trapped.

Waiting. Hoping. Twisting themselves into knots trying to earn a future no one can promise.

Real hope is something else entirely.

FALSE HOPE VS. REAL HOPE

False hope says:

"If I love them enough, they'll change."

"If I do everything right, they'll see the light."

"If I wait long enough, this pain will go away."

It's fragile.

It's dependent.

It sounds spiritual, but it's really just fear with a pretty face.

Real hope, on the other hand, says:

"I'm going to get better, no matter what they choose."

"I'm not waiting on a breakthrough. I'm building a life worth living—today."

"Even if they never change, I can."

"God is still here. And I'm still standing."

WHAT IF THE STORY ISN'T OVER?

Your loved one is still breathing.

That means the story isn't over.

They may be far gone.

They may be deep in it.

They may have burned every bridge.

They may be months—or years—from any kind of real change.

But they are still here.

And that means that *anything* is possible.

Just not on *your* timeline.
Not through your strategies.
Not by clinging harder.

Sometimes, the only way the story begins to change
…is when you stop trying to write it for them.

HOPE IS NOT A STRATEGY—IT'S A POSTURE

Hope isn't what you do to make yourself feel better.

It's how you stand in the middle of the storm.

It's not passive.
It's not desperate.
It's not optimistic fantasy.

Hope is gritty.
It's grounded.
It's rooted in a deep knowing:
"I don't know how this ends,
but I will not surrender my soul to despair."

That's hope.

YOU'RE ALLOWED TO BELIEVE IN REDEMPTION

You are allowed to believe in healing.
You are allowed to believe that miracles happen.

You are allowed to believe that people come back from the brink.

And…

You are allowed to stop trying to *force* that outcome.

Redemption doesn't come through control.
It comes through surrender.
Not the passive kind—but the brave, muscular, wide-open kind.

The kind that says:
"I am not God.
I cannot save them.
I will no longer live like I can."

"I will grieve.
I will heal.
I will live."

"And if they one day return,
I will greet them from a place of strength, not exhaustion."

HOPE FOR YOU

This chapter is not just about hope for them.

It's about hope for *you.*

Because your life matters.
Your healing matters.
Your future is not a side plot in someone else's drama.

You were never meant to live stuck in someone else's disease.

You are allowed to:

- Feel joy again.
- Laugh again.
- Dream again.
- Connect again.
- Find purpose again.
- Say "this ends with me"—and mean it.

You're not waiting anymore.
You're not managing anymore.
You're not hoping for the old version of your family to reassemble.

You are waking up.
And that alone is reason to hope.

SECTION FOUR
LIVING FREE

Finding your own healing, purpose, and identity beyond their addiction.

CHAPTER 13

REBUILD YOUR LIFE WITHOUT WAITING

When families begin this journey, they're typically in survival mode.

They've been stuck in cycles of fear, manipulation, guilt, and emotional whiplash for years—sometimes decades.

So when the storm starts to break—when boundaries are set, detachment begins, and truth is spoken—there's often a strange silence.

And into that silence creeps a question:

"Now what?"

- "What do I do with my time if I'm not checking on him?"
- "What do I talk to my spouse about if we're not managing her crisis?"
- "Who am I, if I'm not trying to save someone?"

The answer is both terrifying and liberating:

You get to build a life. A real one. Starting now.

DON'T WAIT FOR THE PERFECT MOMENT

So many families live in *emotional limbo*—holding off on joy, rest, or new beginnings until the addicted loved one gets better.
"When she finishes treatment…"
"Once he's really serious…"
"After this next milestone…"
"If he stays clean for a year…"

But here's the truth:

You've already lost enough time.

You don't need permission.
You don't need the all-clear.
You don't need things to settle before you take your next step.

You need to *start.*

Even while it's messy.
Even while it hurts.
Even while the future is uncertain.

Because your life doesn't need to be on hold just because theirs is off track.

WHAT DOES "REBUILDING" ACTUALLY LOOK LIKE?

This isn't about grand gestures or reinvention.
It's about doing small things with sacred intention.

Start here:

- **Make plans.** Dinner with friends. A weekend getaway. A class you've always wanted to take.
- **Reinvest in your marriage.** Have hard conversations. Laugh together. Heal the distance addiction created.
- **Reconnect with your healthy kids.** Let them know they matter too—not just the one who's been in crisis.
- **Reclaim your mornings.** Set boundaries with your phone. Journal. Move your body.
- **Find a rhythm.** Routine brings safety. Safety brings breath. Breath brings clarity.
- **Seek joy again.** Not in spite of the pain—but *right through it.*

Your healing isn't a single moment.

It's a way of life.

STOP CHECKING THE SCOREBOARD

One of the most destructive habits in families of addicted persons is constant tracking.

- "How many meetings has she been to this week?"
- "Was that a slur in his voice or is he just tired?"
- "He said he's doing okay, but I don't know…"
- "Did you hear from her today?"

Every interaction becomes a report. Every update, a referendum on whether you're "allowed" to feel safe or not.

This is emotional bondage.

And it doesn't help them—or you.

You are not their probation officer.

You are not their therapist.

You are not their higher power.

You are a human being with your own sacred path.

Stop checking their progress to justify your peace.
Let your peace be unconditional.

FIND SOMETHING BIGGER THAN THIS PROBLEM

Addiction becomes all-consuming.

Eventually, even the family starts orbiting around the disease like it's the sun—everything else becomes secondary.

You need something bigger.

Something that anchors you beyond their recovery status.
- A purpose.
- A calling.
- A spiritual life.
- A creative pursuit.
- A community of people who *aren't* stuck in crisis.

You need to remember who you are apart from this struggle.

Because the person you were before all this?
They've changed.

But the person you're becoming now—that person has depth. Power. Clarity. Wisdom. Fire.

Let them rise.

YOU DON'T OWE YOUR PAIN TO ANYONE

Sometimes families feel guilty for healing.

They say things like:

- "It feels wrong to be happy when she's still out there."
- "If I stop worrying, I'll feel like a bad parent."
- "We should all be suffering—he's still struggling."

But you don't need to match their misery.

You don't need to carry the weight to prove your love.

You are allowed to *choose peace even when they choose chaos.*
You are allowed to *begin again, even if they haven't.*
You are allowed to *live, even if they still haven't chosen life.*

THE NEW WAY FORWARD

You can rebuild your life, one breath at a time:

- From truth, not fear.
- From boundaries, not guilt.
- From freedom, not fixation.
- From peace, not performance.
- From love, not loss.

This isn't about pretending the pain never happened.
It's about honoring the pain by letting it change you—for good.

No longer shaped by reaction.
But by *intention.*

No longer trapped in the story of their downfall.
But rising in the story of your own rebirth.

The world needs that version of you.
And so do you.

CHAPTER 14

FORGIVE YOURSELF FOR NOT KNOWING SOONER

There's a pain most families carry that rarely gets voiced.

It sounds like:

"How did I not see it?"

"Why did I let it go on for so long?"

"How could I have been so blind?"

"What kind of parent lets this happen?"

"How many times did I believe a lie when deep down, I knew better?"

It's the quiet, crushing guilt of hindsight.

And if you're not careful, it becomes a life sentence.

So here's what you need to hear, maybe more than anything else in this book:

You are allowed to forgive yourself.

Not later. Not someday.

Now.

YOU DIDN'T FAIL

You loved someone who was sick.
 You believed someone who was lying.
 You held on longer than most people ever would.

That's not failure.
 That's human.

It doesn't make you stupid.
 It doesn't make you weak.
 It doesn't mean you weren't doing your best.

In fact, most people never even get close to the kind of fierce, sacrificial love you've shown.

But that love doesn't mean you deserved what happened.
 And it doesn't mean you have to carry shame for choices made in the dark.

HINDSIGHT IS A LIAR

Hindsight makes it all seem so obvious:

- "I should've pulled the plug back then."
- "We never should've let her move back in."
- "That intervention should've been the last chance."
- "We knew better. We just didn't act."

But here's the truth:

You didn't know what you know now.
 You weren't who you are now.

You were surviving.
 You were scared.

You were hoping this time would be different.

That doesn't make you a fool.
That makes you family.

And the fact that you've evolved doesn't mean your past self was broken.
It means they were doing their best with the tools they had.

SHAME WILL NOT MAKE YOU STRONGER

Families sometimes think they *need* guilt.
That it keeps them from repeating mistakes.
That it keeps them accountable.
That it proves they care.

But guilt is not the same thing as growth.

Shame doesn't protect you—it *paralyzes* you.

It's the voice that says:
"You're not allowed to heal. You haven't earned it."
"Don't forget how badly you messed this up."
"You let them down. You don't get to move on."

But here's what shame *doesn't* say:

- That you learned.
- That you grew.
- That you fought like hell.
- That you're still standing.

Shame doesn't tell the whole story.
It just repeats the worst parts, on loop.

You get to break the loop.

HOLD YOUR PAST SELF WITH COMPASSION

Picture the version of you from five years ago. Ten years ago. Last year.

See them standing in the middle of the chaos.
    Confused. Afraid. Tired. Hopeful.

Now say this:
    "You didn't know.
    You were trying.
    You weren't ready.
    You loved them.
    And I forgive you."

Because if you keep punishing your past self, you'll never trust your future self.

Healing requires compassion.
    And that compassion has to start at home.

THE ONLY THING YOU NEED TO OWN IS TODAY

You don't need to fix the past.

You just need to stop dragging it with you into every decision.

You don't need to punish yourself for not acting sooner.

You just need to act differently now.

You don't need to explain every misstep, justify every compromise, or atone for every time you chose comfort over truth.

You just need to *decide who you are now.*

That's it.

That's freedom.

FORGIVENESS IS A SPIRITUAL ACT

This isn't just emotional work.
It's *sacred* work.

Forgiveness—real forgiveness—isn't something you earn.

It's something you *receive.*

You are allowed to let go.
To lay it down.
To say:
"God, I didn't know.
I didn't see.
I was afraid.
But I trust that You saw me.
And I trust that You still do."

If grace is real, then it's real for *you*, too.
Not just for the addicted loved one.
Not just for the ones who get it right the first time.

For you.

Especially you.

THE NEW STORY

The old story was:
"I should've done more. I failed."

The new story is:

"I didn't know—but now I do.

I was afraid—but now I'm learning to act.

I was tangled up in their life—but now I'm rebuilding mine.

I was surviving—but now I'm healing."

And I will not keep punishing myself for the time it took to learn.

I will bless that version of me.

And I will walk forward—clear, grounded, and forgiven.

CHAPTER 15

DON'T GO BACK TO SLEEP

There's a strange moment after the hardest part of a crisis passes—when things calm down, when the addicted loved one is no longer active, or when the family has finally made the break.

You're exhausted.
But you're also more awake than you've ever been.

You see clearly.
You speak truthfully.
You know what's yours to carry and what's not.

But here's the danger:
Clarity fades.
Sleep returns.
Old patterns sneak back in, dressed like comfort.

And slowly—quietly—you start to drift.

THE PULL OF OLD ROLES

You may not even notice it at first.

- One favor.
- One check-in.
- One emotional compromise.
- One more time extending grace with no accountability.
- One more stretch of the boundary you said was non-negotiable.

And then suddenly, you're back.

Back in the role you worked so hard to leave:
The Fixer. The Manager. The Emotional Sponge. The Financial Safety Net. The Walking-on-Eggshells Peacemaker.

It happens fast.

Because those roles weren't just habits.
They were *identities*.

And identity doesn't go quietly.

WHAT GOT YOU THROUGH THIS WON'T KEEP YOU THERE

The version of you that woke up in the middle of the crisis—who started speaking truth, setting boundaries, grieving honestly, and reclaiming your life—*that version must be protected*.

Because there will come a moment—maybe many—where you're tempted to slide back into what's familiar.

- When the addicted loved one seems better.
- When the family wants things to "go back to normal."
- When it's just easier to say yes.

But the truth is:

There is no "back to normal."
There is only forward.
And forward requires vigilance.

DON'T TRADE PEACE FOR PREDICTABILITY

The old way was predictable.

You knew your role.
    You knew their reactions.
    You knew the rhythms of crisis, collapse, and temporary relief.

But peace is different.

Peace is unfamiliar.
    It's quiet.
    It can even feel lonely at first.

And without meaning to, you may find yourself creating drama, looking for chaos, or re-inserting yourself—just to feel useful again.

That's not peace.
    That's addiction in disguise.

You don't need to feel needed to be whole.
    You don't need to be in the middle of it all to feel connected.

You need to *stay awake.*

REMEMBER WHY YOU CHANGED

When the temptation to slide back comes, remember this:

- The sleepless nights.
- The lies.
- The manipulations.
- The financial wreckage.
- The destroyed trust.
- The lost time.
- The fractured relationships.
- The moment you said, "Never again."

Hold that moment close.

Not to stay bitter.
   But to stay *awake*.

Because relapse isn't just something the addicted person struggles with.
   Families relapse, too.

Into denial.
   Into fantasy.
   Into control.
   Into rescue.

So stay sharp. Stay humble. Stay grounded.

And if you slip?
   Forgive yourself—quickly—and come back to what's true.

YOU DON'T OWE THE OLD SYSTEM ANYTHING

The people who were comfortable with your silence will struggle with your truth.

The people who benefitted from your exhaustion may not celebrate your peace.

That's okay.

You are not here to keep the old system running.

You are here to live a new way.

You don't owe anyone your old identity.

You don't owe anyone the old version of yourself.

Let them adjust.

Or let them go.

But don't go back.

CHAPTER 16

THIS WAS NEVER JUST ABOUT THEM

You came here because of someone you love.

You stayed because something in *you* needed to change.

Maybe you didn't know that at first.

Maybe you thought this book would help you fix them—finally.

Maybe you were still hoping for a formula, a breakthrough, a shortcut.

But what you've learned is deeper.

There is no shortcut.

There is no formula.

There is only this:

A family gets well the moment they stop waiting.

The moment they stop rescuing.

The moment they start telling the truth—about the addicted loved one, yes,

but even more about themselves.

THE STORY YOU THOUGHT YOU WERE IN

You believed you were in a story about addiction.

The broken son.
    The spiraling daughter.
    The family's fall from normalcy.
    The desperate hope for a comeback.

You believed that if you could just hold on long enough, sacrifice enough, control enough, love enough—it would turn out okay.

But the story you were *actually* in?
    It was always about your awakening.
    About what you had to let go of.
    About the lies you believed.
    About the patterns you participated in.
    About the courage it takes to become someone new.

WHO YOU ARE NOW

You are no longer asleep.

You've learned to sit in discomfort instead of fixing it.
    You've learned to speak the truth without begging someone to receive it.
    You've learned to let go of outcomes, so you could hold on to peace.

You're not perfect.
    You're not always sure.
    But you're *honest* now. And that's everything.

You've stopped being the emotional firefighter.

You've stopped organizing your life around their potential.
You've stopped confusing suffering with loyalty.

And in doing so…

You became free.

IF THEY COME BACK

Maybe one day, the person you love will return—sober, clear, and changed.

If they do, you'll greet them not as someone desperate for a reunion, but as someone whole.

You won't need to explain all you've learned.
They'll feel it.

They'll feel your steadiness.
They'll feel your peace.
They'll feel your integrity.

And if they haven't done the work themselves?
They'll feel your boundaries too.

This time, you won't contort.
This time, you won't beg.
This time, you won't try to rescue them with your goodness.

You'll stand where you are. And they'll have to rise to meet you.

IF THEY DON'T

Maybe they don't come back.

Maybe they don't change.

Maybe they continue on a path that breaks your heart, over and over again.

That doesn't mean this was for nothing.

Because this was never just about whether they make it.
This was about whether *you* would.

And you did.

You chose clarity.
> You chose peace.
> You chose dignity.
> You chose to stop being consumed by a battle that wasn't yours to win.

You chose life.

THE WORLD NEEDS YOU NOW

Your story isn't over.

In fact, it may just be beginning.

Now, you have something most people don't:
> A hard-earned peace.
> A soul that's been through the fire and came out stronger.
> A truth you didn't just learn—you *lived.*

And that kind of clarity? That kind of experience?

It's meant to be *shared.*

Not in performance. Not in preaching.
> But in presence.

- With other families just waking up.

- With friends stuck in denial.
- With strangers who look just like you did five years ago.

You don't have to teach them.
>You just have to *be real*.

And that will be enough.

THE FINAL WORD

You've tried everything.
>Now try living.
>Now try letting go.
>Now try telling the truth—and standing in it.

You're not here to fix anymore.
>You're here to *become*.

And you already have.

So breathe.

Stand tall.

And walk forward.

This time, *you're free*.

YOU'RE NOT ALONE

If you've made it this far, I want to say something simple—and true:

I'm proud of you.

This is not an easy book to read.

It tells the truth. It asks hard questions. It invites you to look at yourself, not as the cause of someone else's addiction, but as someone with power—real power—to change the atmosphere in your home and the rhythm of your own life.

Most families I work with didn't arrive at this place overnight.

They spent years in survival mode.

They begged, bargained, and bent their own boundaries and values in the name of love.

They held on so tightly to someone else's chaos that they forgot who they were without it.

Maybe that's your story, too.

But something's different now.

You're not holding your breath for them to change.
You're beginning to breathe for yourself.

You're not waiting on them. You're waiting on you.

And now—finally—the waiting is over.

That doesn't mean the pain disappears.
It doesn't mean things magically fall into place.
It means that today, you begin to reclaim what addiction tried to steal:
Your voice.
Your clarity.
Your peace.
Your God-given right to live a life anchored in truth and love.

You get to set boundaries—not as punishment, but as protection.
You get to stop rescuing—not out of spite, but out of wisdom.
You get to tell the truth—not to control, but to be free.

Will you get it right every time? No.
Will it be uncomfortable? Often.
But will it be worth it?
Always.

There are thousands of families walking this path alongside you—choosing clarity over confusion, choosing courage over comfort.
You are not alone in this journey.

So keep going.
Keep standing.

Keep choosing truth—even when it's hard.

Keep choosing love—even when it looks different than what you imagined.

And if no one has told you this lately:

You're doing better than you think.

And you're not doing it alone anymore.

WHAT I COULDN'T SAY THEN— A LETTER TO MY FAMILY

From Who I Was Then,

To Who You Are Now

If I could go back—if I could say it plain—this is what I'd tell you:

I wasn't trying to hurt you.

I didn't wake up each day wondering how to lie better, manipulate harder, or drag you down with me.

I was drowning.

I just didn't know how to ask for help without losing the little pride I had left.

The truth?

I needed boundaries.

I needed you to stop saving me.

I needed you to stop making excuses for me.

I needed to hit the wall—not because I deserved to suffer, but because it was the only thing loud enough to wake me up.

But you couldn't know that.

You were loving me the best way you knew how.

And I used that love. I weaponized it.

I turned your loyalty into leverage.

Your softness into shelter.
Your fear into control.

There were moments you saw through me—moments you tried to draw a line.
And I punished you for it.
But I also needed it more than I could say.

I didn't need more chances.
I needed a reason to change.
And I needed to believe that *you* were going to be okay, even if I wasn't.

If I'm telling you the truth—God's honest truth—it's this:
The day you stopped chasing me, I began to look for myself.
The day you said, "No more," something broke in me—and it was the part that kept me sick.
The day you let go…
Was the day I began to want to hold on.

So here's what I'd say, if I could stand in front of you now:
Thank you.
For every boundary I cursed.
For every tear you cried.
For not giving up on the person I could become—while refusing to rescue the one I insisted on being.

You didn't save me.
But you showed me something true.
That love doesn't always say yes.
That peace doesn't always look like harmony.
That sometimes, the most Christ-like thing you can do…
is walk away with grace.

And if your person hasn't come back yet—if they're still lost—
I'll say this:
  Keep living.
  Keep choosing truth.
  Keep becoming the kind of whole that gives them a reason
  to rise.
  And know this with all your heart:
  God never wastes pain.
  He didn't waste mine. And He won't waste yours either.

With gratitude deeper than words,

—Brook

ACKNOWLEDGMENTS

To the families who allowed me to walk beside them—this is yours as much as mine.

To my mentors, teachers, and colleagues who modeled what it looks like to lead with clarity and compassion—thank you for sharpening me.

To my wife, Tracy—thank you for your strength, your love, and your belief in me even when I didn't believe in myself. You are the heart of everything that matters.

To my sons, Maxwell and John Briggs—your presence in my life is the greatest reminder of what's worth healing for.

To my parents and my brother—you lived through more than you ever should have had to. I hope this work redeems even a small part of what was lost.

To Bryan and Michelle—thank you for loving me like a son, for your unwavering support, and for the quiet strength you've brought to my life and family.

To David Elliott—thank you for your vision, your integrity, and for creating a place where the impossible becomes possible. Your legacy changed my life.

And to God—Who never stopped pursuing me, even when I wasn't ready to be found—thank You.

ABOUT THE AUTHOR

BROOK MCKENZIE is a Licensed Chemical Dependency Counselor with over a decade of experience guiding families through the emotional and spiritual chaos of addiction. He is a member of the American Counseling Association (ACA), the National Association for Alcoholism and Drug Counselors (NAADAC), and the Texas Association of Addiction Professionals (TAAP).

Brook's work blends clinical knowledge with personal experience, offering families not just professional insight—but real, hard-won clarity about what actually works. Known for his direct and compassionate voice, he helps families make difficult but necessary changes that can shift the entire trajectory of recovery.

He lives in Texas with his wife and two young sons, and finds purpose in fatherhood, faith, and the everyday joy of living a full, sober life rooted in truth, accountability, and love.

If you'd like to stay connected, learn more, or reach out personally, visit: brookmckenzie.com

May God bless you, guide you, and give you the strength to keep showing up—for yourself, and for the ones you love.